The TEACHER I WANT TO BE

LEARNING AND SHARING THE WORD OF GOD

WORKBOOK

DANIEL L. AKIN

SAMPSON
RESOURCES

4887 Alpha, Suite 220 • Dallas, Texas 75244 • (972) 387-2806 • (800) 371-5248 • FAX (972) 387-0150
www.sampsonresources.com info@sampsonresources.com

HOW TO USE THIS WORKBOOK

The Teacher I Want to Be workbook is designed to accompany the 6-lesson video curriculum by Daniel L. Akin. Each lesson includes a PERSONAL WORD by Dr. Akin; the OUTLINE of his video presentation—with blanks to fill in; a SUMMARY by Dr. Akin; REVIEW, DISCUSSION, BIBLE STUDY/BIBLE TEACHING EXERCISE, APPLICATION and PRAYER. Hopefully, all participants will join in lively discussion and interaction. Ideally, everyone should have a workbook to use in the study and to keep as a valuable reference for years to come.

PART ONE consists of three lessons dealing with how to study the Bible. It is ideal for current and prospective teachers, as well as those who simply want to know how to study the Bible more effectively, but do not plan to teach.

PART TWO consists of three lessons that deal specifically with how to teach the Bible. Again, current and prospective teachers who have already completed the first three lessons of part one will continue and complete these three lessons.

A beautiful "Certificate of Completion" is available for all who complete *The Teacher I Want to Be.*

NOTE: PART THREE is a separate series of 8 to 10-minute micromessages by Dr. Akin entitled SECOND-MILE MOMENTS *Going Above and Beyond for Authentic Teaching.* They are designed for ongoing training and refresher activity. A discussion guide is included in the kit and downloadable from *The Teacher I Want to Be* product page at www.sampsonresources.com.

All Scripture References—English Standard Version (ESV)

TABLE of CONTENTS

PART 1

HOW TO STUDY THE BIBLE

Lesson 1

FOUNDATION: How Do I Get Started?

An Overview of the Interpretive Process

A PERSONAL WORD

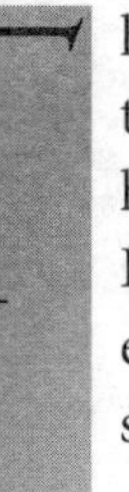

The late Frances Schaeffer reminds us that "God is a talking God and has revealed Himself through His Word." He is a God who delights in communicating with His people, and He has done so in both His living Word—the Lord Jesus Christ—and His written Word—the Bible. Essential to good communication is knowing the right questions to ask, and having eyes that see and ears that hear. This is crucial when it comes to rightly hearing God as He speaks to us through the Bible.

The Bible is a wonderful gift from God and the only dependable source of truth in all the world. Now you know why I'm so passionate about helping people learn to study the Bible! And I'm not talking about just preachers and seminary students. I teach every week in my local church because I want all believers to love God with their minds as well as their hearts. That's what Jesus teaches us in Matthew 22:37. He wants our hands and feet to follow our heads and hearts in joyful obedience to what we read, study and come to understand.

If we compare studying the Bible to riding a bicycle, we understand that the more we do it, the better we will be at it! But just as we must learn to ride a bicycle correctly, we must learn to study the Bible correctly, and I want to share some principles that will help you get the most out of your study time. As you begin to use these principles, you will discover more about God and His plans for you than you ever dreamed possible! You'll probably find yourself wanting to share with others what you've learned.

LESSON OUTLINE

ESSENTIAL COMMITMENTS FOR BIBLE STUDENTS AND TEACHERS

I. A COMMITMENT TO A HIGH VIEW OF SCRIPTURE

A. Jesus had a high view of Scripture. Matthew 5:17-18

B. The apostles had a high view of Scripture. 2 Timothy 3:16-17

C. The Holy Spirit guarantees our high view of Scripture. 2 Peter 1:20-21

D. There is sufficient evidence to prove that the 66 books of our Bible are authentic, inspired writings from God through His chosen authors.

II. A CONVICTION OF THE ________________________ OF ALL SCRIPTURE

A. The Bible is our authority for daily living.

B. No one area of the Bible is any more inspired than another.

1. The words of Jesus are no more authoritative than the words of Paul.
2. The epistles are no more inspired than the genealogies of the Old Testament.
3. There is equal inspiration, but there are different degrees of importance.

C. All interpretation and teaching must be wedded to the Scriptures, not rooted in something else, e.g., reason, experience, traditions.

III. A CALLING TO RIGHTLY DIVIDE THE WORD OF __________________________

A. Only what God says is truly important.

B. We must work (study) hard to accurately apply Scripture to daily life. 2 Timothy 2:15

IV. A COMMITMENT TO APPLY THE INSTRUCTION OF SCRIPTURE

A. We must go beyond reading the Bible and actually do what it says. James 1:22-25

B. Interpretation must give way to application, or the process is incomplete.

V. A WILLINGNESS TO BE CONFINED TO THE AUTHOR'S ___________________________

A. Scripture may have multiple applications but only one meaning.

B. The health of our churches depends on a strict interpretation of Holy Scripture.

Scripture is the foundation of the Church: the Church is the guardian of Scripture. When the Church is in strong health, the light of Scripture shines bright; when the Church is sick, Scripture is corroded by neglect; and thus it happens that the outward form of Scripture and that of the Church usually seem to exhibit simultaneously either health or else sickness; and as a rule, the way in which Scripture is being treated is in exact correspondence with the condition of the Church. —Walter Kaiser, *Toward an Exegetical Theology* (quoting John Albert Bengel)

The Church and the Scripture stand or fall together. Either the Church will be nourished and strengthened by the bold proclamation of her biblical texts or her health will be severely impaired.... Should the ministry of the [Word] fail, one might just as well conclude that all the supporting ministries of Christian education, counseling, community involvement, yes, even missionary and society outreach, will likewise soon dwindle, if not collapse. (Walter Kaiser, pgs.7-8)

THE BIBLE IS ONE "BIG STORY" WITH MANY "LITTLE STORIES."

I. THE BIBLE HAS A GRAND AND GLORIOUS NARRATIVE THAT HELPS FRAME OUR INTERPRETATION AND LEAD TO A BALANCED THEOLOGY.

II. THE BIG STORY HELPS US BETTER UNDERSTAND THE LITTLE STORIES.

A. See the "Big Story" from ______________________________.
Example: Creation → Fall → Redemption → New Creation

B. See the "Big Story" from ______________________________.
Example: God → Sin → Christ → Response

FIVE KEY QUESTIONS THAT HELP INTERPRETATION

1. What does this text teach me about ____________?
2. What does this text teach me about fallen humanity?
3. How does this text point to Christ? *(John 5:39, 46; Luke 24:25-27, 44-47)*
4. What does God want me to ______________?
5. What does God want me to do?

THEOLOGICAL CATEGORIES LOCATED IN THE TEXT

1. Revelation
   - General
   - Special
2. Theology Proper
   - Creation
   - God
   - Angels
4. Christology
5. Soteriology (salvation)
6. Pneumatology (the Holy Spirit)
7. Ecclesiology (the Church)
8. Eschatology (the future)

SUMMARY

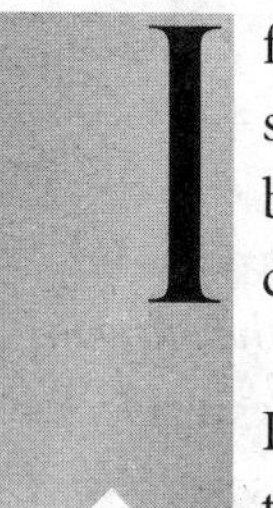

If I have hit the bull's-eye with this lesson, you're feeling challenged to go deeper in your personal Bible study habits; and if you stick with it, you'll soon be studying the Scriptures with increased confidence. I believe you will also grow stronger in your convictions and better equipped should you ever decide to become a Bible teacher.

Let's keep in mind that our goal is to serve the body of Christ for the glory of God and the good of the nations. How we treat the Bible is of the utmost importance if we are to serve with passion and excellence. Now we're off to a good start, but there's much more to come! Let's get into some discussion now.

REVIEW (Make sure blanks in outline are filled in properly.)

DISCUSSION

1. Take a few moments to discuss as a group why you decided to participate in this study. What would you like to gain from it?

2. When you were growing up, what role did the Bible play in your home? Did it play a prominent role or was it just "there" and not spoken of much? Was it missing altogether? Why do you think people own Bibles—sometimes even the latest translations—but often don't read them?

3. Is there a difference in *reading* the Bible and *studying* the Bible? Why not just read it and let that be enough? After all, reading is better than nothing. Why *study* it? Discuss as a group.

4. The key to success in most anything is "getting started." Whether it's a diet, a remodeling project, putting in a new flower bed, a fitness program—whatever—things begin with a decision that's followed up with action. The key is "*what* motivates you to make the *decision* and then keeps you following through once you've made it." Discuss some of the factors that lead a person to make the *decision* to start studying the Bible after years of not studying it. Can life experiences be a factor?

5. Why do you think people find it hard to make time to read—much less study—the Bible? Are they too busy? Find it to be hard work? Don't know how to get started? Don't understand what they read? Don't think they need it? Share your thoughts.

6. If we tried to list all of the benefits and blessings we receive from knowing and studying the Scriptures, the list would be endless! Take a moment to list and discuss a few of the benefits and blessings you receive from the Bible. Be specific.

BIBLE STUDY EXERCISE

Take a few minutes to look at the scripture passage below and answer the "five key questions for interpretation." Read the text at least three times to gain deeper insight before answering the questions.

Joshua 1:7-9 *Be strong and very courageous. Be careful to obey all the law my servant Moses gave you; do not turn from it to the right or to the left, that you may be successful wherever you go.* [8] *Keep this Book of the Law always on your lips; meditate on it day and night, so that you may be careful to do everything written in it. Then you will be prosperous and successful.* [9] *Have I not commanded you? Be strong and courageous. Do not be afraid; do not be discouraged, for the Lord your God will be with you wherever you go.*

Question #1: What does this text teach us about God?

Question #2: What does this text teach us about fallen humanity?

Question #3: How does this text point us to Christ?

Question #4: What does God want me to know?

Question #5: What does God want me to do?

APPLICATION

- From this point on, when reading and studying various Bible passages, ask yourself the "five key questions for interpretation" we covered in the exercise above.
- Review this lesson in the days ahead as you spend time in Bible study. Watch for the "big stories" and main ideas to help you see the passage in a fresh new way.

Father, thank You for the Bible and for the privilege of coming to know You as my personal Lord and Savior through its message. I am determined to study it more and apply its teachings in every area of life. Please call me out when I'm not following through consistently as I should. In Jesus' name, Amen.

PART 1

HOW TO STUDY THE BIBLE

Lesson 2

OBSERVATION: What Do I See?

A PERSONAL WORD

God has given us a book that reveals His wisdom and His perspective on things. We call it the Bible. This book is like no other book that has ever been or ever will be written. It is truly one of a kind, and it is one of God's greatest gifts to the human race.

Unfortunately, we get so busy we tend to neglect the Bible and make decisions based on our own understanding. Have you ever been around someone who knew bits and pieces of the Bible but didn't really understand any of them? That's why it's important that we improve our skills in observing what the Scriptures really say. Adrian Rogers was noted for saying that "a text out of context is a pretext"—that is, an excuse to do something or say something that is not accurate. I agree with him completely.

Get ready to become a better student of the Bible. Again, as Francis Schaffer noted, "God is a talking God and has revealed Himself through His Word." It's exciting to know that He is talking to us! And as we listen, we will so fall in love with the Bible and the Christ of the Bible that we won't be able to get enough of it!

LESSON OUTLINE

WHY STUDY THE BIBLE?

I. IT IS THE MEANS TO DEVELOP SPIRITUAL MATURITY AND GODLY WISDOM.

"Godly wisdom" is the ability to see life from God's perspective and react or respond to it with His mind. (Hebrews 5:11-14; Phil. 2:5)

II. SCRIPTURE IS THE PRIMARY MEANS OF SPIRITUAL GROWTH

Our aim as believers should be to be like Jesus. After all, this is why God gave us the Bible. (1 Peter 2:2; Romans 8:28-30)

III. THE BIBLE GIVES THE ONLY GUIDELINES TO FOLLOW TO PRESENT OURSELVES TO GOD IN A MANNER APPROVED OF BY HIM. (2 Timothy 2:15; Romans 12:1-2)

IV. ALL SCRIPTURE IS PROFITABLE. (2 TIMOTHY 3:16-17)

A. *For Doctrine* – what to ______________________

B. *For Rebuke* – what ______________________ to believe

C. *For Correction* – how not to ______________________

D. *For Training in Righteousness* – how ______________________ live.

V. THREE BASIC SKILLS WE MUST DEVELOP

When we study the Bible, we must read it right and read it well. Here are three skills that will help us:

A. Observation – "What do I ______________________?"

B. Interpretation – "What does it ______________________?"

C. Application – "How does it ______________________?"

THE FIRST MAJOR STEP IS *OBSERVATION* – "WHAT DO I SEE?"

I. DEVELOP THE ABILITY TO SEE AND DETERMINE WHAT THE TEXT SAYS.

Observation is taking a good hard look at what is in the text.

A. Learn to read intelligently, intentionally, and interactively.

B. Two helpful principles for reading the Bible

1. Learn to read the Bible as if this is the first time you've seen the text (Often it's good to read from different translations).

Translations for Teaching	Translations/Paraphrases for Reading
ESV (English Standard Version)	NIV (New International Version)
NASB (New American Standard Bible)	NLT (New Living Translation)
HCSB (Holman Christian Standard Bible)	THE MESSAGE
NKJV (New King James Version)	CEB (Common English Bible)
KJV (King James Version)	AMPLIFIED BIBLE
	GNB (Good News Bible or Translation)

2. Learn to read the Bible as a love letter (personal).

C. We need to read the Bible.

1. ______________________________
   a) Repeatedly (3-5 times)
   b) Lengthy portions in one sitting
   c) Starting at the beginning

2. ______________________________

D. Read the Bible and repeatedly ask six questions.

1. Who?
2. ______________?
3. When?
4. Where?
5. ______________?
6. How?

E. As we read, we are to read:

1. ______________ - Recall God's promises and claim them.
2. Imaginatively - Identify with it.
3. ______________ - Meditate; take time.
4. Purposefully - Actively expect to be transformed.
5. Acquisitively - How can I hold on to it?
6. Telescopically - Read in light of the whole.

II. WE NEED TO LEARN WHAT TO LOOK FOR.

To *see* the text is to observe what information God has put in a biblical passage. See the details and seek meaning from those details. Make all possible observations from a text.

A. Look for key terms, e.g., the verbs, significant words, concepts, repetition, etc.

B. Look for atmosphere.

C. Observe ________________________. Some kinds of relationships you will observe are:

1. Grammatical relationships
2. Logical relationships
3. Chronological and/or geographical relationships
4. ______________________ relationships
5. Contextual relationships
6. Relationships in *genre*. Here are some of the basic kinds of literature that are found in the Bible, and many interpretive mistakes could be avoided if we would honor the *genre* of a text.
   a) Teaching
   b) Narratives
   c) ______________________________
   d) Parables
   e) ______________________________
   f) Prophetic
   g) Apocalyptic

SUMMARY

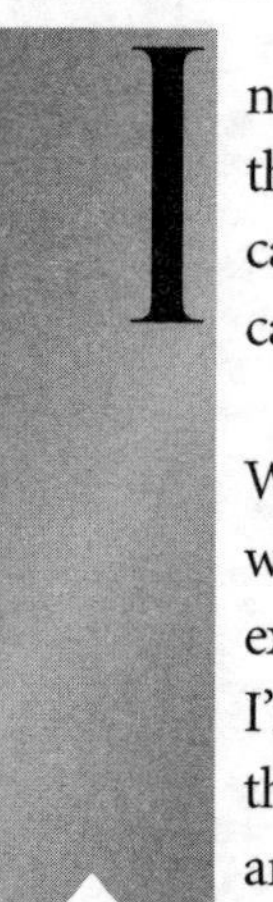

In this lesson we have affirmed our faith in the completeness and infallibility of the Bible—we have confessed that it is profitable to teach us how to live—we have learned that accurate observations of the Bible are critical—and we have learned that we must understand the text *objectively* (what it means in principle) before we can do anything with it *subjectively* (what it means to *me* personally).

Whether you're just beginning to study the Bible or are an experienced student of the Bible, I suggest starting where you are, applying this lesson one step at a time. Take it slowly, methodically and prayerfully. No one is expecting you to become a scholar overnight. I've been a student and teacher of the Bible for many years, and I'm still struggling to learn and grow myself. But as you develop in your ***observation*** skills, you will discover the depths of meaning God has given you in His Word. Like learning to ride a bicycle—you started out slowly and carefully, then gradually learned to go faster and more confidently—you will experience the exhilaration of knowing God more intimately as you study His Word. As you read and study the Bible, be observant and ask yourself: *"What do I see?"*

REVIEW (Make sure blanks in outline are filled in properly.)

DISCUSSION

1. The terms "spiritual maturity" and "spiritual growth" can mean different things to different people. Think about what they mean to you and then talk about how the Bible helps you grow spiritually.

____

____

2. Take a few moments to discuss what you believe Paul means by "an approved workman" in 2 Timothy 2:15. Do you feel like you qualify as a "workman"? Why or why not? How does the Bible help us become "approved workmen"?

3. To say that life in today's culture is "demanding" and that time is more valuable than ever is almost an understatement! How does a person find the time to read the Bible "thoughtfully, repeatedly, patiently, reflectively, etc."? Discuss the various Bible reading schedules and study habits of the group and jot down some ideas.

4. The Bible includes a variety of genres or categories, e.g., teaching, narratives, poetry, parables, miracles, prophetic, apocalyptic. Share with the group which of these mean the most to you and why. Your experience may encourage others.

5. If you were to create a yearlong study plan for your group, which genres would you include and why? Would you choose particular books regardless of the genre?

BIBLE STUDY EXERCISE

Asking six simple questions of the text will lead us toward stronger interpretation of Scripture. The questions are: *Who—What—When—Where—Why—How*? After reading the passage below and answering the six questions, discuss your thoughts.

John 4:1-26

Who are the characters in the passage?

What is the context of the passage?

When did the event occur?

Where did it take place?

Why is this passage important?

How was the passage communicated?

APPLICATION

- Reflect on the six questions you should repeatedly ask when reading a passage of Scripture—who—what—when—where—why—how? Apply this principle to the study of Matthew 28:19-20.

- Pick one of your favorite passages of Scripture and read it from a translation or version you're not familiar with—and read it as if you've never read it before. Various translations are available online in websites such as www.biblegateway.com. As you read, ask yourself, "What do I see?"

Father, I realize that I cannot just read the Bible and understand it without careful observation and thought. I want more than a head-knowledge of what I'm reading. I want a heart-understanding of the truth as You intended, and I want to embrace it with my life. Thank You for Your Word. In Jesus' name, Amen.

NOTES

PART 1

HOW TO STUDY THE BIBLE

Lesson 3

INTERPRETATION: What Does It Mean?

A PERSONAL WORD

We are on an incredible journey—learning how to study the Bible. It's like an adventure that never ends, filled with unlimited rewards and hidden treasures just waiting to be discovered! I cannot imagine there being a single day in my life when I decide that I no longer want to study this wonderful book given to us by God. I hope you feel the same way, and I hope your joy grows as we continue this study. Today's lesson is a subtle shift from seeing what Scripture *says* to understanding what Scripture *means.*

Have you ever had an "Aha!" moment in your life when you fully grasped something that has been staring you in the face for a long time? I remember hearing the story of Abraham and Isaac on the mountain of sacrifice for many years and being inspired by Abraham's willingness to obey God. But the first time I saw the fuller meaning of the event (the picture of Christ on the cross), I couldn't contain my excitement! I jumped up out my chair and ran around looking for someone to tell!

The desire of my heart is for you to have a lifetime of "Aha!" moments! That's one of my goals in helping you learn to interpret the Bible correctly. Let's get to it!

LESSON OUTLINE

THE PROCESS OF BIBLICAL INTERPRETATION

(How to "C" the Bible Accurately)

Hermeneutics is the "science and art of interpretation." It is a *science* because it follows certain rules—it is an *art* because it takes practice to develop it. Hermeneutics is also the study of methodological principles of interpretation that allow us to take what we see and determine what it means.

THREE TRUTHS TO REMEMBER

1. It takes time to expose oneself to the brilliance of revealed truth and digest it.
2. There is more truth in the Bible than we can grasp in one or many readings. Infinite, eternal truth has this nature.
3. It takes practice and experience to hone the necessary skills to develop an understanding of a biblical text with accuracy.

SEVEN BASIC "C" PRINCIPLES OF INTERPRETATION

1. Content – That which is actually before you in the text.
2. ____________ – Beginning to bring together the pieces of your observations.
3. Context – What goes before and after (there is both a *near* and a *far* context).
4. Comparison – Comparing Scripture with Scripture.
5. ______________ – The social setting of the time.
6. Consultation – Use of reliable resource tools (after you have done personal study).
7. Construction – Building a sound teaching outline that arises clearly out of the text.

TEN INTERPRETATIVE RULES FOR UNDERSTANDING THE BIBLE

Just as the Bible interpreter must properly use the right tools, he or she must also observe some simple rules if accurate interpretation is to take place. Remember, hermeneutics is both an art and a science; it is a science because there are rules and principles.

1. Work from the belief that the Bible is authoritative, that it is the very Word of God.

2. Interpret difficult passages in the light of clear passages. Let the Bible interpret itself.

3. Interpret personal experience in the light of Scripture and not Scripture in the light of personal experience.

4. Remember that Scripture has only ____________ intended meaning (deposited by its author) but _______________ applications.

   a. One meaning (sense)
   b. Many applications (significance)

5. Interpret words and passages in harmony with their meaning in the time of the author. Pursue the literal, natural, normal meaning of the text according to its genre or literary type.

   a. A text cannot mean today what it did not mean originally.
   b. A text cannot have a different meaning from the one of the author. However, it may have a fuller and more complete meaning (called "sensus plenary") than the human author originally understood.

6. Interpret Scripture in light of its progressive ______________________________.

7. Remember, you must understand the Bible grammatically before you can understand it theologically.

8. A doctrine cannot be considered ______________________ unless it includes all that Scripture says about it.

9. Distinguish between the proverbs and the promises of God.

10. When two doctrines taught in the Bible appear to be contradictory, accept both as scriptural in the confident belief that they resolve themselves in a higher unity.

THE VARIOUS CONTEXTS OF A TEXT

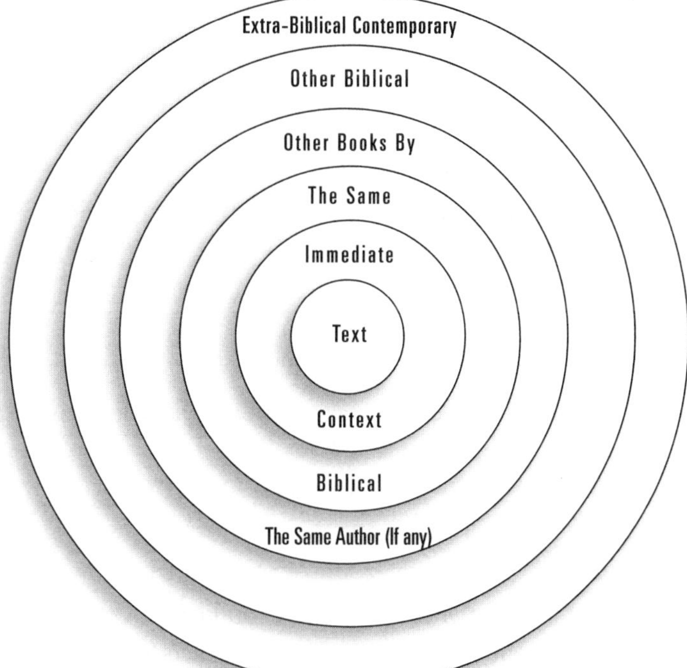

ANALYZING THE TEXT

1. Pray, asking the Holy Spirit for help.
2. Track the ____________________.
3. Look for key words needing definition.
4. Look for repetition of phrases and words.
5. Look for ___________________ in the text that will form the number of points and the nature of the teaching outline.
6. Note the near and far context.
7. Search for helpful and supporting Scripture (cross references).
8. Craft what you see as the ____________________ idea of the text (MIT).
9. Write out any and all observations and applications you see in the text.
10. Examine your study aids and write out any helpful insights (note the source for future reference and appropriate citation).
11. Look for the ____________________ the text logically supports.
12. Submit your study to the "five key questions" that honor the "Big Story."

SUMMARY

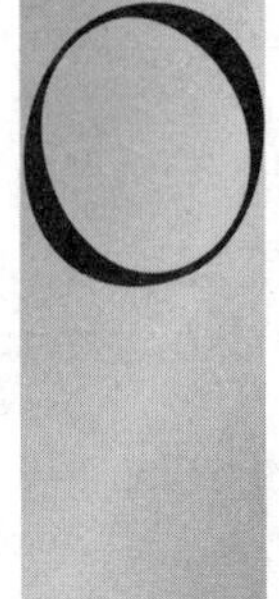

Obviously, interpreting Scripture correctly isn't the easiest thing in the world, but with training, patience and practice, you can learn to do it well. Don't be intimidated by the task. Continue to review this lesson as many times as needed until you feel comfortable with the principles. Eventually, they will become natural to you.

None of us will ever perfectly master interpreting the Bible, but we will grow and enjoy much satisfaction working toward it. Don't get bogged down with the Bible's most difficult passages either. There are dozens of good commentaries and helps. And keep in mind: Some passages are so difficult that Christianity's best scholars don't always agree! Just remember that it's okay to tell someone you aren't sure about the meaning of a particular passage, and then go study it some more. You will benefit greatly in the long run. Now let's get going with some discussion!

REVIEW (Make sure blanks in outline are filled in properly.)

DISCUSSION

1. How do you feel about the fact that the Bible has more truth in it than we can ever learn? Does it bless you or frustrate you? Share your thoughts with the group.

2. What resource tools have helped you most in Bible reading and study? What commentaries, dictionaries, maps, visual aids, etc., do you use regularly? How do they help you?

3. Firmly stated in the video lesson was this statement: "Scripture has authority over anyone's personal experience. In other words, God will not give you a thought or experience that contradicts Scripture." How do you feel about this statement? Have you ever experienced something that seemed to contradict Scripture? How were you able to reconcile the issue?

4. Consider the roles of prayer and the work of the Holy Spirit in helping us understand Scripture. How does the Holy Spirit help us, and what should we ask for in prayer as we study a passage? Try to be specific.

BIBLE STUDY EXERCISE

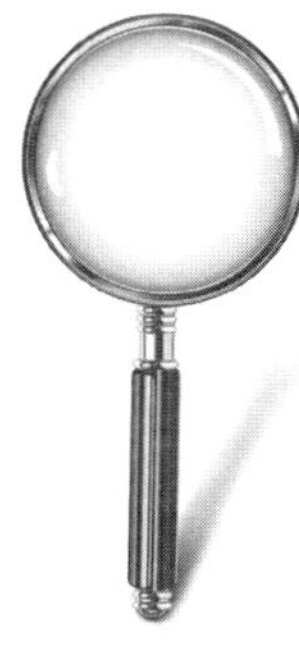

Two of the seven "C's" in interpretation are *content* and *context*. Some of the misunderstandings in Bible study come as a result of focusing only on the *content*, but ignoring the *context* of a passage. Read the following passage and answer questions that relate to *content* and *context*.

Philippians 4:10-13 [10] *I rejoiced in the Lord greatly that now at length you have revived your concern for me. You were indeed concerned for me, but you had no opportunity.* [11] *Not that I am speaking of being in need, for I have learned in whatever situation I am to be content.* [12] *I know how to be brought low, and I know how to abound. In any and every circumstance, I have learned the secret of facing plenty and hunger, abundance and need.* [13] *I can do all things through him who strengthens me.*

1. This is a much-loved passage that ends with the often-quoted verse 13. What is the context or situation in which Paul is writing to the Christians at Philippi?

2. Now read the passage again. What is Paul saying in verses 10-12?

3. In light of the context of the passage (4:10-13), what do you think is the main idea of 4:13?

4. How easy is it to read something into the passage that the author never intended if we do not consider both the content and the context?

APPLICATION

Practice the rules of interpretation by choosing a familiar Bible story or passage and identify the following:

1. Verbs: _____
2. Key Words: _____
3. Repeated Phrases/Words: _____
4. Main Idea: _____
5. Possible Applications: _____

Father, I confess that interpreting the Bible is serious business, and I don't want to get it wrong. Help me to lean on You for understanding, discernment, and humility. I pray that Your Holy Spirit will teach me so I can share with others. In Jesus' name, Amen.

This concludes PART 1 – HOW TO STUDY THE BIBLE.
Continue with PART 2 – HOW TO TEACH THE BIBLE.

PART 2

HOW TO TEACH THE BIBLE

Lesson 4

APPLICATION: How Does it Work in Real Life?

A PERSONAL WORD

I'm so excited that you have chosen to continue in this study because it means you are already a teacher or maybe considering becoming one. Far too many Christians are like the Dead Sea—lots of good, valuable resources flowing in but nothing ever flowing out. Why would anyone want to live like that? Instead, let's turn the corner in this series by learning to teach others what the Bible says and means, and how what it says and means should affect the way we live.

By the way, I want you to know just how much I value Bible teachers. If you are a teacher, you are extremely important in your church, but you are just as important in your home and community. We need people teaching the Bible in every setting imaginable and to every age group possible. Let's dive in now and find out how Bible truths really work in everyday life!

LESSON OUTLINE

SIX STEPS TO ACCURATE APPLICATION

Howard Hendricks says that application is simply "Clothing truth with overalls!"

CRUCIAL PRINCIPLE TO REMEMBER

Application is always built on interpretation.
If the interpretation is wrong, the application will be wrong. 

I. BE AWARE OF THE problems WITH APPLICATION.

A. Some teachers of the Bible stop the interpretive process before it is complete!

B. We substitute Knowledge for life-changing experience.

C. We like to apply Scripture to areas we are already working on and neglect new avenues of need.

D. We rationalize the process to fit our present lifestyle. Behavior can effect belief.

E. We allow an emotional experience to be substituted for a volitional decision.

F. Pressures from society cause us to compromise what we know to be true.

G. Our prejudice and spiritual truth come into conflict.

H. Ignorance – We cannot apply what we do not know.

II. BRIDGE THE INTERPRETIVE HORIZON FROM THE BIBLICAL WORLD TO OUR WORLD.

A. Begin to move from the then of the text to the now of your audience.

B. The interpretation must be correct for the application to be correct.

III. KNOW YOUR APPLICATIONAL CONTEXT OR SITUATION.

Remember: The interpretation is *one*, but the applications are *many*.

A. Know yourself. (1 Timothy 4:16)

B. Know your people—age, background, needs, etc. We should look to the original audience of the text, then to ourselves, then ask four key questions:

1. How are we like them?
2. How are we unlike them?
3. How should we be like them?
4. How should we be unlike them?

IV. STATE YOUR APPLICATION IN THE FORM OF A UNIVERSAL PRINCIPLE.

A. You are looking for truth anywhere, anytime, anyplace and under any circumstance.

B. Be in line with the needs, interests, questions, and problems of today. This is the key to relevance.

THERE ARE TWO HISTORIES, AND YOU MUST BRIDGE THE HORIZONS.

ORIGINAL HISTORY		OUR HISTORY
Philippi A.D. 60-63	*Philippians*	*Your City / Your time*
Truth revealed out of the "then"	Between two worlds universal truth emerges	Truth reborn into the "now"

C. Be in harmony with the general tenor of Scripture. Never forget the analogy of faith: Scripture is Scripture's own best ______________________.

D. Be specific enough to indicate a course of action. Fifteen questions to ask:

1. Is there an ______________ for me to follow?
2. Is there a sin to avoid or confess?
3. Is there a promise to claim?
4. Is there a ______________ to repeat?
5. Is there a command to obey?
6. Is there a condition to meet?
7. Is there a verse to memorize?
8. Is there an ______________ to avoid?
9. Is there a challenge to face?
10. Is there a principle to apply?
11. Is there a habit to change, start or stop?
12. Is there an ______________ to correct?
13. Is there a truth to believe?
14. Where is Christ?
15. Where is the Gospel?

V. SATURATE YOUR MIND IN TERMS OF RELATIONSHIPS.

A. Christianity is best understood as a series of new relationships.

B. Consider your existing relationships and look for specific ways to apply the text.

VI. CONSCIOUSLY PRACTICE ON YOURSELF BEFORE APPLYING TO OTHERS.

"What we live is what we believe. Everything else is just so much religious talk." **— Vance Havner**

A. You cannot adequately apply to others what you have not applied to yourself.

B. You cannot be diligently applying everything, but you should be consciously applying something.

C. Two Questions:

1. What am I trusting God for right now?
2. What is my plan of action?

APPLICATION QUESTIONS: HOW SHOULD THE TEXT AFFECT MY . . .

1. . . . attitudes toward God, others, circumstances?
2. . . . knowledge of God?
3. . . . Behavior? (Habits to develop, habits to change, habits to confirm)
4. . . . relationships? (Where do I need to forgive, seek forgiveness, encourage, rebuke, submit, lead?)
5. . . . Motives? (Am I doing right for the wrong reasons?)
6. . . . values and priorities? (Who or what comes first? Who or what *should* come first?)
7. . . . character?

SUMMARY

It has been said that knowledge without application produces arrogance and pride. Trust me: One of the best ways I know to stay humble is to be a Bible teacher! Once you put on the "teacher hat," you begin to realize just how little you know compared to the vast wealth of knowledge and wisdom found in the Bible.

Teaching will keep you humble if you do a good job of applying truth to your own life first. But the good thing is that humility will radiate to those you are trying to teach. In fact, it will *draw* them to you. The combination of knowledge and humility is a valuable attribute of any teacher or leader.

Be comforted knowing that you are well on your way to reaching your potential. Observing and interpreting Scripture naturally leads us to make application of its meaning, but still there is much more to come. When you package what we've talked about in a format that instills confidence, you will be ready to communicate more effectively and powerfully!

REVIEW (Make sure blanks in outline are filled in properly.)

DISCUSSION

1. Think about your past experiences in Bible studies and classes. Have the classes focused more on *learning* about the Bible or on *doing* what the Bible says? When was the last time you left a Bible study determined to take some action because of the lesson? Describe that situation to the group.

2. As we discussed earlier, our culture is constantly tempting us to compromise the truths we clearly see in Scripture. If we give in to this temptation, how will it affect the application we bring out in our lessons? What are some biblical truths that you feel are being challenged most in today's culture?

3. Describe how participants can influence the application you bring out of a particular text. If you were teaching on Jesus raising Lazarus from the dead, what application would you bring to seasoned senior adults in Sunday school or life groups versus 2nd graders in vacation Bible school?

4. In your opinion, what does it mean for a lesson to be "relevant"? What keeps a lesson from being relevant, and how can you avoid being irrelevant? Discuss this as a group.

____

____

5. We can all agree that every good lesson should contain a meaningful application to life. But even if we make the application, how can we be sure our audience has received it and will follow through? List some things we will see if the Bible truths we're teaching are being applied in the lives of our people.

1. ______________________________________
2. ______________________________________
3. ______________________________________
4. ______________________________________

BIBLE TEACHING EXERCISE

Building application into your lesson is vital to moving the class from being *hearers* of the Word to *doers* of the Word. In this exercise let's consider a few of the "15 questions to ask of the passage" as you prepare to teach. Your answers should reflect your thoughts on the passage.

Luke 6:46-49 46 *Why do you call me "Lord, Lord," and not do what I tell you?* 47 *Everyone who comes to me and hears my words and does them, I will show you what he is like:* 48 *he is like a man building a house, who dug deep and laid the foundation on the rock. And when a flood arose, the stream broke against that house and could not shake it, because it had been well built.*[a] 49 *But the one who hears and does not do them is like a man who built a house on the ground without a foundation. When the stream broke against it, immediately it fell, and the ruin of that house was great.*

Are there examples to follow? ______________________________

Is there a sin to confess or deal with? ______________________________

Is there a promise to claim? ______________________________

Is there a command to obey? ______________________________

APPLICATION

- After you prepare your next lesson, leave it for a while, then come back and read it with fresh eyes. Ask yourself, "How do I expect people to respond to this lesson? What difference will the lesson really make?" After answering, evaluate the quality of your application and adjust as necessary.

- Select a familiar Bible passage and focus on the "then/now bridge" to help your audience make proper application. Use this exercise frequently to become an effective "bridge builder."

Lord, I don't want to teach just so people will ***know*** *more about You and Your Word. I want them to* ***do*** *more,* ***serve*** *more and* ***share*** *more. Help me apply each lesson to myself first so that I can teach with authenticity and humility. I want to be an example of what I teach so that Christ will be glorified through me. In Jesus' name, Amen.*

NOTES

PART 2

HOW TO TEACH THE BIBLE

Lesson 5

PRESENTATION: How Do I Put It All Together?

A PERSONAL WORD

Congratulations! You've soaked up much in these first four lessons, and I know the Lord is going to use you to bless others. As much joy as there is in studying God's Word and growing personally, there's even more joy teaching others and seeing the Bible take up residence in their lives. In the flesh, I might boast about holding a position in a seminary—but, honestly—I'm more fulfilled seeing God using men and women I have taught over the years now leading their own respective ministries. This far surpasses any position I or anyone might hold in an educational institution.

Here's the challenge for today's lesson: We don't just want to learn to communicate God's Word—we want to learn to communicate it *effectively.* We're going to try to help you put your observations, interpretations, and applications into such a neat little package that anyone could pick up your lesson, compare it to the biblical text, and readily agree that you are on target. Now don't underestimate the power of the "neat little package" idea. After all, dynamite could be described that way! A lot of power in a little stick! Let's learn how to put together this package so you can light the fuse and expect a powerful outcome the next time you teach!

LESSON OUTLINE

OUTLINING YOUR STUDY OF GOD'S WORD: AN OVERVIEW

1. Pray, asking God for His help through the ministry of the Holy Spirit.
2. Let your interpretation of the text drive and determine the teaching outline.
3. Have as many major points as the text naturally demands (locate the seams).
4. Make sure ______________ ______________ and sub-points (if you use them) arise clearly and naturally out of the text. Be able to see your outline in the text.
5. State your points in the present tense and in complete sentences. Be clear, concise, and true to the text.
6. Make your points the application of the message. Let them inform, instruct and inspire your people as to what they should learn and do.
7. Make sure your major points connect with the title and the main idea of the text (MIT) and the main idea of the message (MIM).
8. Make sure your __________-______________ connect with the major point they support.
9. Do not overload your people with more than they can intellectually digest! "You should always have more in your warehouse than you put in your shop window."
10. Cover and fill the skeleton of your outline with the meat and marrow of the observations and interpretation of the biblical text.
11. Write out your study, merging all aspects of your preparation with a view of exalting our Lord and edifying your audience here and now.
12. Practice reading the ________________ ______________ repeatedly and out loud.

MODEL: PHILIPPIANS 2:1-11

Main Idea of Text (MIT): Jesus demonstrated true humility in His incarnation and crucifixion.
Main Idea of Message (MIM): Pursue the mind of Christ as revealed in His incarnation and humiliation.

THE MIND OF CHRIST: A HUMBLE PASSION

Philippians 2:1-11

I. CULTIVATE THE CHARACTER OF CHRIST. 2:1-5

A. Enjoy Divine Blessings. 2:1

B. Exhibit Divine Behavior. 2:2-4

1. Let Your Life Be Characterized by ______________. 2:2
2. Let Your Life Be Characterized by __________________. 2:3
3. Let Your Life Be Characterized by ___________________. 2:4-5

II. SEE THE HUMILITY OF CHRIST. 2:5-8

A. See His Humility in His Renunciation. 2:5-6

B. See His Humility in His Incarnation. 2:7

C. See His Humility in His Crucifixion. 2:8

III. REJOICE IN THE EXALTATION OF CHRIST. 2:9-11

A. Accept His Exalted Position. 2:9

B. Acknowledge His Exalted ____________________. 2:10

C. Adopt His Exalted Confession. 2:11

WHY IS OUTLINING SO IMPORTANT?

1. It is foundational for effective communication.
2. It is helpful for understanding the text.
3. It is important because the human mind seeks unity.
4. It is important because the human mind seeks ____________.
5. It helps us know how we have arrived where we are and where we want to go.
6. It helps us gain a proper perspective on the text we are studying.
7. It helps us discover the pattern, order, or logic of the biblical author.
8. It helps us isolate the __________ __________ of the biblical author (MIT).
9. It helps us identify points or thoughts in the text (different from the MIT) as well as the sub-points which explain and amplify the main points.

A SIMPLE GUIDE FOR GOOD OUTLINING

I. A WELL-DEVELOPED OUTLINE HAS STRUCTURE.

A. The main points are the central ideas designated by Roman numerals (I, II, III, etc.).

B. Sub-points are the points that explain the main topics designated by capital letters, (A, B, etc.) They are subordinate to the main point, amplifying, supporting, or illustrating the main point.

II. THE PASSAGE OUTLINE SHOULD HONOR THE __________________ OF THE BIBLICAL AUTHOR.

III. AN EFFECTIVE OUTLINE DEALS WITH COMPLETE IDEAS AND NOT PARTIAL THOUGHTS OR FRAGMENTS.

A. Make each point in the outline a __________________________ sentence.

B. Usually you should use declarative or imperative statements instead of questions when outlining. The point of the outline is to explain and apply the text, not develop questions. (There are, however, legitimate exceptions to this principle.)

C. Each point should usually be a _________________ idea. Avoid the use of compound and complex sentences.

IV. EACH MAIN POINT THAT HAS SUB-POINTS WILL USUALLY HAVE AT LEAST TWO SUB-POINTS.

SUMMARY

Now let's face it: You fall into one of two camps—1) people who like to outline or 2) people who don't like to outline. Whichever one you are, let me encourage you to just **do it**! The more you outline, the better you will get at it, the easier it will be, and the more you will appreciate the process. Remember how you learned to ride a bicycle! You stayed with it!

Learning to outline well isn't just so your material will look good on paper or make a good handout for your group. To the contrary, as you will see in our final lesson, outlining will help you become a better communicator. And isn't that a worthy goal? Simply stated, outlining your lesson will help you be the prepared teacher you want to be. Listen to these profound words of Howard Hendricks from his book *Teaching to Change Lives*:

> "Preparation is the best insurance you can take out on your communication. In preparation, you give your message form and features. Your message needs structure; it needs to be packaged, and the ability to package your message is what separates the men from the boys and the women from the girls in communication."

Outlining reflects preparation, structure, orderliness and a plan for teaching. I don't know about you, but I need all the help I can get!

REVIEW (Make sure blanks in outline are filled in properly.)

DISCUSSION

1. Now that you've seen a good model of outlining, what do you think about it? How does this compare to the way you normally prepare a lesson? Is this outline method easier or more difficult? Share with the group.

2. We often hear teachers say, "I have more material to cover than I have time for." Is this true of you? If so, how do you make the lesson work? Will outlining your lesson help relieve tension or heighten tension? Discuss together.

3. Before we get into the next lesson on communication, let's get specific about how outlining might enhance your teaching? What do you think? Will it help or hinder? Can you make it work? If not comprehensive outlining, what about at least partial outlining? Talk further about it.

4. Have you listened to an entire lesson or sermon and at the end of it wondered what the person was talking about? If so, how did it make you feel? What were your thoughts about the speaker? (Careful now!) What about the concept of clearly communicating the "main idea" of the passage or lesson and how doing so impacts participants in the group? Talk about how you're making this work in your teaching.

BIBLE TEACHING EXERCISE

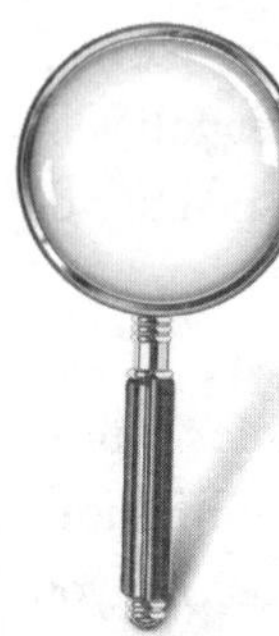

Outlining a passage can be one of the most helpful tools in a teacher's toolbox. In doing so, it's a good idea to look for natural breaks in the text that can indicate natural places for points and sub-points. Open your Bible to Colossians 3:5-4:6. The major points are provided in the outline below, so all you need to do is fill in the sub-points. Discuss with the group what you come up with.

EXPERIENCING THE SUFFICIENCY OF CHRIST (Colossians 3:5-4:6)

I. EXPERIENCE HIS SUFFICIENCY IN THE INDIVIDUAL (3:5-17)

  A. Removing the ____________ Self (3:5-11)

  B. Putting on the ____________ Self (3:12-17)

II. EXPERIENCE HIS SUFFICIENCY IN THE HOME (3:18-4:1)

  A. Wives and ______________________ (3:18-19)

  B. Children and ______________________ (3:20-21)

  C. Slaves and ______________________ (3:22-4:1)

II. EXPERIENCE HIS SUFFICIENCY IN RELATIONSHIP WITH OTHERS (4:2-6)

  A. Church's Relationship with ________________ ________________ (4:2-4)

  B. Church's Relationship with ________________ (4:5-6)

Preparing your lesson using a simple outline of main points and subpoints like the one above will give you a clear, concise structure within which to organize your content.

APPLICATION

- Now it's your turn to practice outlining. Choose a favorite Bible story or passage of Scripture and outline it according to the model presented in this lesson.

- Bring your outline to the next meeting and exchange it with one of the other group members. Ask them to constructively critique your outline, then you do the same for them.

Father, I want to be organized in my preparation and teaching so I can communicate clearly the truths of Scripture. Help me be accurate in my teaching so Your Word will impact the hearts and minds of those I teach in a lasting way. In Jesus' name, Amen.

PART 2

HOW TO TEACH THE BIBLE

Lesson 6

PROCLAMATION: How Do I Communicate Effectively?

A PERSONAL WORD

Think about the long list of people God entrusted to proclaim His message throughout history. A few names that come to mind are Moses, David, Jeremiah, Daniel, Paul, Peter, James, John and many more. We will all agree that the most prominent of all messengers is Jesus Christ Himself. In contrast, however, God even used a donkey as His mouthpiece. The point is that *your name* goes on this same list, not in the sense of proclaiming newly inspired material, but nevertheless, as an important part of the divine plan to take the Gospel to the nations and teach people to observe His commandments.

In the first five lessons of this study I have tried to build a foundation that enables us to take this final step to become more effective communicators of the Bible message. We have learned how to understand content so we can impact the minds of our participants; we have seen a simple model that organizes us to challenge the will of our participants; and now we can focus on an effective delivery of the message so that the hearts of men, women, boys and girls will be touched and compelled to live their lives for the glory of God.

What an incredible thought that God could use us to influence others and see positive change come about in their lives! Now, don't get me wrong—we can't *change* anybody! But God can use us as instruments to bring about change in others. We can teach, but we can't force people to learn and apply what we're teaching. Let's commit to being the best preparers, the best proclaimers, the best communicators and the best examples we can be as teachers! I'd like to share some thoughts with you on how to do that!

LESSON OUTLINE

TEN ESSENTIAL SKILLS

A word fitly spoken is like apples of gold in a setting of silver. (Proverbs 25:11 ESV)

What you say is more important than how you say it, but how you say it has never been more important than it is today! (Akin)

Effective teachers of the Bible come with varied experiences, backgrounds and abilities. There is no "one-size-fits-all" model. Since your goal is to teach God's Word in the best possible way, here are ten essential skills you'll want to work on:

1. Find your ____________________ and optimal delivery.
2. Give attention to your style.
3. Dress appropriately for the occasion.
4. Know the importance of your ____________________.
5. Know your audience.
6. Give attention to your voice.
7. Become a ________________________.
8. ________________________ your listeners in your teaching.
9. Use humor appropriately and effectively.
10. Use ________________________ as you are able, as it is readily available, and as is appropriate.

FINAL THOUGHTS

1. Get better by watching and listening to others who communicate well.
2. Get better by watching and listening to yourself. Yes, it may be painful!
3. Get better by practice! Teaching in front of a mirror is a time-tested technique!
4. Get better by asking for and receiving helpful feedback.
5. Remember the ___________________________ of Ecclesiastes 12:9-14.

> *Besides being wise, the Preacher also taught the people knowledge, weighing and studying and arranging many proverbs with great care. The Preacher sought to find words of delight, and uprightly he wrote words of truth. The words of the wise are like goads, and like nails firmly fixed are the collected sayings; they are given by one Shepherd. My son, beware of anything beyond these. Of making many books there is no end, and much study is a weariness of the flesh. The end of the matter; all has been heard. Fear God and keep his commandments, for this is the whole duty of man. For God will bring every deed into judgment, with every secret thing, whether good or evil.* Ecclesiastes 12:9-14 (ESV)

SUMMARY

Thank you for completing this series and for investing the time and effort to become a better student and teacher of the Bible. I'm sure you would agree that the return on your investment will be well worth your effort. Hold on tightly, though, because there's more to come! As you continue to improve your study, preparation and communication skills, the satisfaction and rewards will pour in—along with the rewards being stored up for eternity!

Let me challenge you to go back through this material several times. There is so much to learn that it will take years to master it! I teach all the time and in all kinds of settings, and I'm still learning! Sure, brilliant minds can memorize lessons and conjure up fancy words, but a genuine concern for people, careful preparation and practice—all based on a life well-lived and a Christ-like example—just can't be beat! Let me close with the words of William Arthur Ward:

"The mediocre teacher *tells.* The good teacher *explains.* The superior teacher *demonstrates.* The great teacher *inspires.*"

REVIEW (Make sure blanks in outline are filled in properly.)

DISCUSSION

1. How would you describe yourself as a communicator? Are you loud, soft-spoken, emotional, authoritative, entertaining, serious, etc.? How does your personality and natural style affect your ability to communicate? If you could change your style to something else, what would you add or subtract?

2. Dress codes have certainly changed a lot in recent years both in the workplace and at church. People have varying opinions on this. Is this worth being concerned about? What's really important here? Talk about it together.

3. What does the term "wordsmith" mean to you? Do you consider yourself a "wordsmith"? What are some ways you could improve your vocabulary and the words you use in your teaching? Share your thoughts with the group.

4. One of the proven facts about teaching and learning is that people learn better if they can participate in the lesson—asking questions, interacting with others, sharing their thoughts and insights. Just sitting and listening to someone talk for 30 or 35 minutes can become boring. How can you involve people in the lesson so they feel like they are contributing rather than just listening or observing? Have you sat under teachers who were "masters" at involving the people in a Bible lesson? Compare notes with others in the group and discuss your thoughts.

5. Think back over this teaching series for a moment. Has any particular lesson spoken to you in a special way? Have any particular points challenged you, motivated you or increased your awareness in some area? Share together.

____

____

6. Finally, to close our study, please complete the following statement: "The teacher I want to be" is one who . . .

____

____

BIBLE TEACHING EXERCISE

We're going to focus now on **reading** the Bible—**out loud.**

Keep in mind that as a teacher, you probably spend as much time reading the Bible out loud to the people in your group as the pastor does to the entire church. How you **read** it is important. You can rush through it—use no expression—no variation of pitch or tone—no distinction between the "voice" of a Pharisee or disciple—you can mumble, garble, hurry—whatever! Or—you can make the scripture passage come alive, reflecting the emotion, personalities, situation, etc., of the passage. Naturally, we're not suggesting that you try to sound overly dramatic—just more authentic within the context of the passage.

Your reading exercise is **John 6:1-14**, the account of Jesus feeding the five thousand. Since several different personalities speak in this passage, your assignment is to read the passage in a way that reflects the different personalities and their take on what's going on around them. Just consider the situation itself! In the minds of the disciples—utter confusion and impossibility! What on earth are they going to do? Consider how they would have expressed themselves given their different personalities. What would Jesus' tone of voice reflect? Desperation and loud proclamation, or firm, quiet confidence? After all, He knew how things were going to turn out.

Also, you'll want to read what Jesus says in a different manner from how you read what Philip says. And you'll want to read John's narrative (story progression) in a different manner from how you read material quoted by the various characters in the passage. In other words, don't read everything in the same "voice" when all those personalities should have a "voice" of their own. Most people read everything in one "voice."

And please, **do not rush your reading**! This is one of the biggest mistakes you can make. Don't look at your watch or clock on the wall and think, "Wow! I've got to hurry through this!" Think about it: *You're telling people what you think the scripture passage is worth.* Instead, be deliberate and take your time when you're reading the Bible out loud!

- In the passage at hand—John 6:1-14—consider the context, the setting, the crowd, the excitement level.
- Discuss how various voices should be read or communicated in this passage and why. Do they communicate anxiety, fear, doubt, joy, peace, relief, jubilation? If so, read that way! If the character is smiling, read with a smile. Whatever you do, avoid a dead-pan, non-emotional voice—unless that happens to be in character at the time.
- If time permits, assign different participants to read the "voices" of John, Jesus, Philip, Andrew, and the crowd (all other participants) out loud.
- Again, you want to be careful not to over-do things, e.g., over-exaggerate, be overly dramatic or cheesy.

NOW READ: If you're in a group, take turns reading portions or all of John 6:1-14. Ask other participants in the group to read certain characters. Afterwards, talk about the experience and how it felt to speak with realism and authenticity the "voices" of Bible characters. How did it feel to hear it? What's to be gained from an exercise like this?

APPLICATION

- Identify some individuals whom you consider to be outstanding communicators and observe them closely with this lesson in mind. Take notes on what they do well, and think about what you can learn from them to improve your own teaching.

- Ask someone you know and trust to read the notes from this lesson and then observe your teaching at an upcoming opportunity. Ask for positive, constructive feedback on your content, involvement of participants and your communication skills. You will probably be surprised at the positive feedback you receive.

Father, thank You for these insights on studying and teaching the Bible. I promise to embrace these truths and principles and make them a part of my thinking and teaching. I am firmly convinced that if I do my part, Your Spirit will enable me to become "the teacher I want to be." In Jesus' name, Amen.

What a joy it has been to share with you a few things I've learned over the years about teaching God's Word. Personally, I can never get enough of it! And I'm still in the process of becoming "the teacher I want to be." Teaching the Bible is my favorite thing in the entire world! I hope it's the same with you. It's not something we "have" to do—it's something we "get" to do! What a privilege it is to convey the life-changing truths of God to those around us, see them come to Christ and join the fellowship of the church. I tell you—it's humbling! And when you consider the message we're delivering, it deserves the best we can offer.

I'd give anything for the chance to meet you in person, know you and hear about your service for the Lord. Even though we may never meet, I'm going to consider you a fellow-servant in the ministry and pray for you across the distance as we serve the Lord together.

Remember what William Arthur Ward said: "The mediocre teacher *tells.* The good teacher *explains.* The superior teacher *demonstrates.* The great teacher *inspires.*" Let's make this commitment together: The teacher you and I want to be . . . is a teacher who does them *all*! With God's help we can do it!

May God bless you and be with you always.

Danny Akin

APPENDIX

Additional Resources and Helps for Bible Study and Teaching

Reference Resources (* – Free resource # – Online resource)

Study Bibles

ESV Study Bible
ESV Study Bible Online#
HCSB Study Bible
HCSB Study Bible Online#*

Bible Dictionaries

Holman Bible Dictionary Online (http://www.studylight.org/dic/hbd/)#*
New Bible Dictionary (IVP)

Commentaries

Bible Speaks Today Series
Tyndale Old Testament Commentary Series
Tyndale New Testament Commentary Series
Warren Weirsbe's BE Series
The Expositor's Bible Commentary
Christ-Centered Exposition Commentary Series
New American Commentary Series
Holman Old Testament Commentaries
Holman New Testament Commentaries
Calvin's Commentaries (http://studylight.org/com/cal/)#*

Other Helpful Resources

BibleGateway.com
Spurgeon's Sermons (http://www.spurgeongems.org/sermons.htm) #*
Desiring God.org#*
Radical.net/media/#*
Daniel Akin.com#*
Studylight.org (→"Bible Study Tools")#*
Preceptaustin.org#*
Grace to You (http://www.gty.org/resources) #*
Gospel Coalition (http://thegospelcoalition.org/resources) #*
Halley's Bible Handbook
Wide Variety of Bible Apps

Resources for Studying and Teaching the Bible

Engaging Exposition by Daniel L. Akin, Bill Curtis, and Stephen Rummage
Faithful Preaching and *Proclaiming Jesus* (e-book) by Tony Merida